#PLAN to WIN tweet Book01

Strategic Territory and Account Planning

By Ron Snyder and Eric Doner

THiNKaha®
E-mail: info@thinkaha.com
20660 Stevens Creek Blvd., Suite 210,
Cupertino, CA 95014

Copyright © 2011 by Ron Snyder and Eric Doner

All rights reserved. No part of this book shall be reproduced, stored in a retrieval system, or transmitted by any means electronic, mechanical, photocopying, recording, or otherwise without written permission from the publisher.

Published by *THiNKaha*®, a Happy About® imprint
20660 Stevens Creek Blvd., Suite 210, Cupertino, CA 95014
http://thinkaha.com

First Printing: August 2011
Paperback ISBN: 978-1-61699-068-8 (1-61699-068-6)
eBook ISBN: 978-1-61699-069-5 (1-61699-069-4)
Place of Publication: Silicon Valley, California, USA
Paperback Library of Congress Number: 2011931459

Trademarks

All terms mentioned in this book that are known to be trademarks or service marks have been appropriately capitalized. Neither Happy About®, nor any of its imprints, can attest to the accuracy of this information. Use of a term in this book should not be regarded as affecting the validity of any trademark or service mark.

Warning and Disclaimer

Every effort has been made to make this book as complete and as accurate as possible. The information provided is on an "as is" basis. The author(s), publisher, and their agents assume no responsibility for errors or omissions. Nor do they assume liability or responsibility to any person or entity with respect to any loss or damages arising from the use of information contained herein.

Advance Praise

"Ron and Eric show, with proven results, how sales professionals can assess and approach their selling landscape with a plan to increase their success. They explain how to implement planning in the most effective way at each stage."

Mari Anne Vanella, Founder & CEO, The Vanella Group, Inc., and Author of *42 Rules of Cold Calling Executives*

"Very impressive integration of planning, strategy, and tactics combined with execution and assessment to close the loop in pursuit of sales growth. I believe that this book provides an excellent roadmap to success for any sales person or sales manager who wants to leverage their time/value to gain maximum positive results."

Owen G. Foster, Senior Vice President, Marketing Resources, Rochester Midland Corporation

---

"In today's selling environment, it's essential to have a plan and make your sales messages timely, personal, and relevant to your territory or strategic accounts customers. This book, written by two experienced sales pros, provides practical ideas that can be implemented quickly by field, phone, and online sales reps and managers alike."

Anneke Seley, CEO and Founder, Phone Works, and Coauthor, *Sales 2.0: Improve Business Results Using Innovative Sales Practices and Technology*

"This book is chock full of 'golden nugget' ideas that can help any B2B salesperson succeed in sales. Pick just one and it can prove to be your 'silver bullet' to closing more (larger) deals. I especially recommend applying the principles to your most important opportunities—those that can make your quarter (or year)!"

Silvia Quintanilla, Principal and Chief Sales Detective, Industry Gems Sales Intelligence

"Action without a well thought out plan, as well as a great plan without focused action, results in driven behavior—not success. *#PLAN to WIN tweet* goes beyond the sales process and provides templates for both—a comprehensive sales plan and the focused action needed to reach your sales goals."

Joan Washburn of Washburn Endeavours, LLC, President of Washburn Endeavours, former Vice President of Sales of PETNET

"This book captures the key components in territory and account strategic planning. In today's sales environment, planning is critical and the most important lesson that I teach our sales team and management team. Ron and Eric provide an excellent roadmap and teaching that is of great value to any sales organization."

Tim Henning, Sr. Vice President, Alliance Imaging

"I love this book. It shows how to properly establish, organize, and execute a plan that will translate into increased sales and profits. This book is a must read for any sales person who wants to be successful. My entire sales team has learned valuable tips from this book that translated into bottom line revenue."

Jeff Musson, CEO, Dynamite Network Solutions Inc.

"There are literally hundreds of great insights in this book and reminders of what we really already know but don't do! It is a practical framework that every sales professional and leader must review regularly if they want to be successful in this new world of selling. My favorite sound bite is 'Hope is not a strategy' and I personally have used Eric's pre-call framework to great effect."

Chris Brown, Co-Founder and CEO, Market Culture Strategies

Dedication

Steven Harper
Sam Haring
Bob Karr
Tim Henning
Jim Jones
Howard Snyder
David Snyder
David Meeting
Mark Miller
Victoria Hibbits
Michael Williams
Dave Asprey
John Reighard
Paul Lansky
Steve Daniel
Joan Washburn
Jim Rohn

Acknowledgments

Terri Snyder

Janet Snyder

Jeff Snyder

Diana Doner

Richard Doner

Fred Klemencic

David Steinore

Mark Smolinski

Mark Stiving

Jack Wolf

Ron Snyder and Eric Doner

Why We Wrote This Book?

Today, selling is more challenging than ever before; technology enables buyers to get information without your involvement, and competitors can easily approach accounts and contacts. You must have a solid plan to add value and stay engaged with your customers. Further, a good plan will enable you to focus your time and resources to produce the best possible results.

We are thriving sales consultants who have served successfully in business-to-business sales and management roles in multiple industries for a combined total of over sixty years. We know from experience how difficult it is to manage sales territories and strategic accounts. Having managed territory and account plans, we've witnessed firsthand the dramatic impact that good planning and effective coaching can have on sales performance.

A compilation of best practices in territory and account management, this book is a guide to help you significantly improve your results. We are sharing with you the essence of our personal experience and our observations from working with thousands of sales people and managers over many years.

If you are an account manager, the material in this book will enable you to:
- Create insightful and achievable territory and account plans
- Enhance existing plans
- Develop and deploy winning strategies to penetrate and retain key accounts
- Manage your territory and time for maximum return

If you are a sales manager/leader, this book will help you:
- Adopt/adapt proven planning tools into current practices
- Train and coach your sales team on proven planning techniques
- Better monitor your sales team's wins and losses
- Enhance/improve your team's sales productivity

How to Read This Book

Each chapter includes:

- An overview, including a clear set of objectives/outcomes you can expect to achieve by acting on the ideas and insights from your reading
- A brief self-assessment—exercises and questions to deepen your understanding and identify actions you can take to improve your results
- Several brief and concise statements ("tweets") that provide actionable insight on the topic

In addition, the Appendix includes tools and references to help you accelerate your results.

Good Reading, Good Planning, and most important, Good Selling!

Ron Snyder *@ronlsnyder*
rsnyder@territoryplan.com
http://www.territoryplan.com

Eric Doner
edoner@achievecorp.com
http://www.achievecorp.com

Contents

Foreword by Bob Karr   11

Section I
Why You Need a Plan   15

Section II
The Key Ingredients   29

Section III
Penetrating Your Territory   45

Section IV
Winning a Strategic Account   61

Section V
Managing Your Territory and Time   77

Section VI
The Role of Sales Management   91

Strategic Territory and Account Planning

Section VII
Executing Your Plan 107

Appendix A: Territory and Account Planning Resources 121

Appendix B: Target Account Selection Criteria 125

Appendix C: Funnel Requirement Formula 127

Appendix D: Territory Planning Template 129

Appendix E: Strategic Account Planning Template 131

Appendix F: Sales Time Log 133

Appendix G: Annual Sales Call Allocation Calculator 135

About the Authors 137

Foreword by Bob Karr

There have been a lot of books written about how to be successful in selling. This book is different because it's written in simple terms that everyone can understand. It is packed with useful ideas and quick tips to help anyone engaged in professional sales. Most important, the authors have clearly spelled out how to develop and implement successful territory and strategic account plans.

This book cuts to the chase. You could spend a lot of time reading textbooks,

Strategic Territory and Account Planning

or you could pick this up and get what you need very quickly. Further, it is full of helpful information to remind experienced sellers of what they once learned, but have not used lately. It is also great for people building their careers and sales approach.

Ron and Eric provide insight "from the trenches" in sales and management roles. And, they've worked with dozens of companies to help dramatically improve sales practices and results.

You can't take shortcuts in the sales process. Ron and Eric have spelled out all the steps. If you follow them and do what they recommend, you will see your sales skyrocket!

Bob Karr
CEO LinkSV

Bob is the CEO/Founder of LinkSV (http://www.linksv.com), a website that connects the dots between the people, capital and companies of the Silicon Valley, and is positioned at the intersection of business intelligence and social networking. He has been an active angel investor, an advisor to emerging Internet companies, and a co-founder of the Angels Breakfast Club. Bob retired from a thirty-year career in the corporate liability insurance business where he spent fifteen years as a Partner of Dinner Levison Company and another fifteen years as SVP of the Sedgwick Group, where he managed Business Development & Client Services focused exclusively on emerging and pre-IPO companies in the Silicon Valley. Many of Bob's emerging clients have turned into successful IPOs.

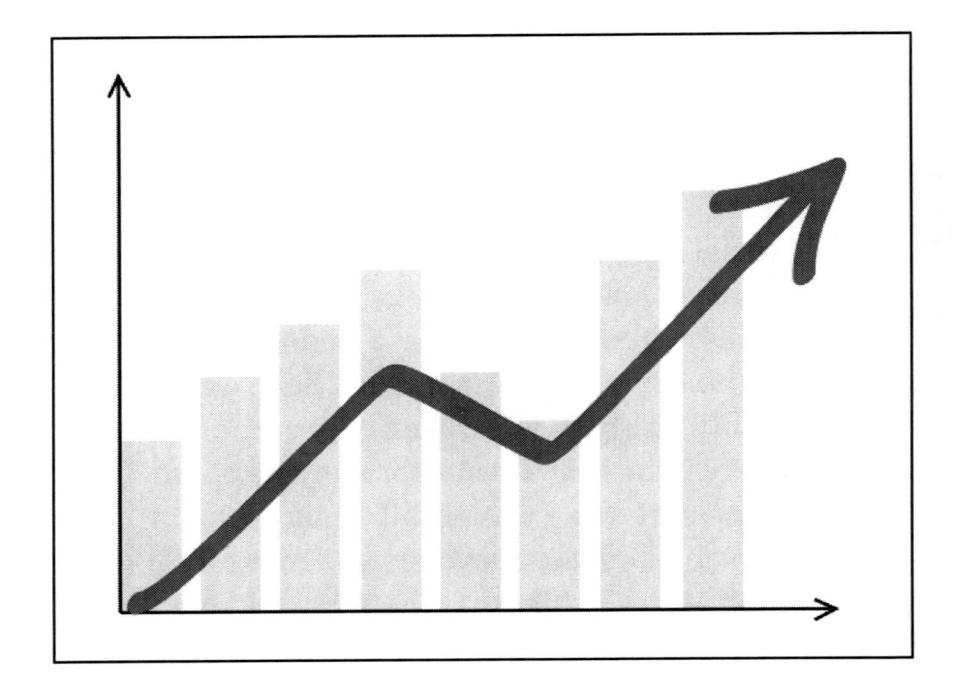

Section I: Why You Need a Plan

Section I
Why You Need a Plan

After reading this section you will be able to:
- Describe the benefits of planning
- Discuss the requirements of planning
- Recognize the consequences of not planning

Without a good plan, you are likely to:
- Overlook opportunities to penetrate your territory or strategic accounts
- Lose sales you could have won and take longer to win new business
- Unnecessarily lower your selling price and reduce your profit margins

Ron Snyder, one of the authors, helped a medical capital equipment company (ADAC Laboratories; now a division of Philips Healthcare) institute a comprehensive approach to sales planning and selling methodology. Within one and a half years, they had the following results:
- Bookings increased forty-three percent
- Margins went up by ten percent
- Market share improved by fifty-three percent
- Productivity per salesperson up by fifty percent
- Win/Loss ratio grew by 131 percent

Having a plan enables you to manage a great deal of complexity. This includes understanding the market, focusing on the customer problems you can solve, selecting your best solution, and managing the internal and partner resources necessary to meet your objectives. It enables you to make the best use of your time and resources by connecting strategy to key tasks. Using your plan, you can ensure that critical tasks are implemented in the time-frame required to win the business. Through it, you give appropriate attention to the critical path—the steps that have the most impact on producing the result on time. Without a plan, it is easy to omit a key element and dramatically compromise your results.

Have you ever had your priorities dictated to you or been told on which accounts to focus your sales efforts? In the absence of a carefully conceived

Section I: Why You Need a Plan

plan, many account managers fall victim to the whims of uninformed executives who perceive opportunities in your territory differently than you do. However, when armed with a good plan, your clear analysis and strategies will prevail.

Success Story: Account Management

Snyder managed a twenty million dollar opportunity for HP, selling to another Fortune 100 company. The sale took eighteen months and involved a wide range of internal resources and customer representatives.

He reflects:

My detailed strategic account plan enabled me to:

1. Identify our competitive advantages.
2. Articulate our value proposition and clearly describe how it met their needs.
3. Make sure our sales, division people, and executive sponsor were on the same page.
4. Manage meetings between a wide range of people from the customer's and our organization.
5. Respond effectively to competitive threats.
6. Keep the sale on track.

I could never have managed the effort, kept everyone engaged and won the business without a clear plan that I updated on a regular basis. The bottom line is that you need a good plan backed with persistent effort to win a complex, competitive business opportunity.

Self-Assessment

- Consider companies you regard as successful, well-managed, high-performing organizations. Can you imagine how they would have performed without a solid business plan?
- Reflect on times when you did not have a plan and/or did not work your plan. What did you miss? What were the consequences?
- Are you a skilled planner? If not, how could you improve your planning abilities?
- Think of the best planner you know. Ask them how they do territory and account planning.

1

"Most people don't plan to fail—
they fail to plan."
-Jim Rohn

2

Understand your customer's
business—better than they do.

Section I: Why You Need a Plan

3

Plan-Do-Win... a good plan and consistent follow-up produces extraordinary results!

4

Without a plan and a process to implement it, sales are accidental.

> **5**
> The more complex and competitive the selling environment and the target account, the more you need a good plan.

> **6**
> Reviewing and reflecting on your plan is where the learning occurs.

Section I: Why You Need a Plan

7

Without a plan, you are just flailing; lost in a morass of action items.

8

Planning is the breakfast of champions… without it, you will waste your time pursuing ineffective strategies.

9

The presence of a clear plan makes it much easier to make decisions and move quickly to win.

Section I: Why You Need a Plan

> **10**
> Manage the critical path; it makes the most difference in reaching the goal on time.

> **11**
> We're all drowning in data, dealing with too much information and need actionable insight.

12

"It's not the will to win that matters...everyone has that. It's the will to prepare to win that matters."

-Paul "Bear" Bryant

Section I: Why You Need a Plan

13

"If you don't know where you are going, any road will get you there."
-Lewis Carroll

14

Having a clear, well thought-out plan improves your probability of success dramatically!

15

Having a clear vision and how to get there enables you to marshal and manage the resources necessary to win.

16

The plan gives you direction and enables you to defend your actions to management and others who question them.

Section I: Why You Need a Plan

17

Though planning may not be glamorous or exciting, it is the key to effective implementation and, ultimately, to success.

18

"If you don't have plans of your own, you'll always fit into somebody else's."
-Jim Rohn

19

The second best plan finishes second. Sometimes it doesn't finish at all.

20

"Anything you clearly imagine, ardently believe and enthusiastically act on must inevitably come to pass."
-Paul J. Meyer

Section II: The Key Ingredients

- ☑ SWOT Analysis
- ☑ Strategy
- ☑ Accounts
- ☑ Opportunities
- ☑ Relationships

Section II
The Key Ingredients

After reading this section you will be able to:
- Describe the critical elements of a territory plan
- Explain the key elements of an account plan
- Discuss and describe each element of a SWOT analysis

Creating and implementing a plan that focuses on high-potential accounts, opportunities, and partners improves sales productivity. According to SiriusDecisions' Research Brief, "Productivity: More Than Just the Topline," improved sales productivity provides:

- More opportunities
- Shorter sales cycles
- Larger sale amounts
- Higher win rates

You need to be sure to cover all of the key items on the territory/strategic account plan checklist. It starts with a clear understanding of what is going on in the territory or strategic account. (See the Territory Planning Template in Appendix D.)

The best way to do this is to conduct a SWOT analysis that carefully examines:

- **Strengths** upon which to build the plan. For example, a unique business model or feature set.
- **Weaknesses** to respond to. A competitor's advantage in market share, product features, or distribution channel is an example.
- **Opportunities** in the marketplace to take advantage of. Think of how your solution meets your buyers' compelling needs.
- **Threats** in the selling environment to beware of, such as competitive moves, changes in technology, industry or regulatory standards.

At this point, conduct an informal competitive analysis to ensure that you understand and aptly respond to your key competitors' offerings. You need to understand why a buyer would delay or resist buying from you.

Section II: The Key Ingredients

With your SWOT and competitive analysis in place, generate your strategy. The first step is to develop your value proposition with genuine differentiators. This is the vehicle for communicating your advantages to prospective customers. This may include technology, customer relationship/advocacy, business model, return on investment (ROI), and response to regulations/industry trends, strong partnerships, and reputation.

Next, you need a clear understanding or the characteristics of high probability prospects/projects to pursue. This will enable you to qualify well and use your time most effectively. (See Appendix B: Target Account Selection Criteria.)

Do the research to uncover the high-payoff accounts and opportunities to pursue in your territory and the best business units and opportunities to pursue in your strategic accounts. This is where you take the strategic perspective you have gathered and make it actionable.

Identify customer and prospect relationships to leverage to drive business. Also, consider which partner relationships you can leverage. This includes strategic and channel partners and more informal relationships you have with other, non-competitive people who call on the same accounts.

Your plan needs to be SMART: Specific, Measurable, Achievable, Relevant (to the market/account), and Time-bound.

When you have done this, ask yourself, "What am I missing (in my territory or strategic account) that would cause my plan to fail?"

Self-Assessment
- Identify your top five strengths or opportunities to leverage.
- Identify your top five weaknesses or threats.
- Clearly describe your value proposition and key differentiators. Make sure it really distinguishes you from your competition. Can you deliver it credibly with conviction?
- Review characteristics of profitable and unprofitable customers and prospects who did not buy and use this to create the short list of characteristics of good prospects.

#PLAN to WIN **tweet**

- Think of recent prospects who suddenly decided to evaluate products in your category. What was it that compelled them to take action?
- Consider three recent sales that you won. From an objective observer's point of view, what could you have done better? How can you build these insights into your plan?
- Review three recent opportunities you lost. Identify one or two things you will do differently next time.

Section II: The Key Ingredients

21

> "Luck is preparation meeting opportunity."
> -Earl Nightingale

22

"Be prepared and you will be lucky"
-The I Ching

23

Insight is the key to powerful planning... know your market, customers, and competition.

Section II: The Key Ingredients

24

Build your plan around the compelling needs of your target audience and you will triumph!

25

To win, you need to understand what is going on in your market, territory, and accounts.

26

Know your value proposition cold and believe it. Your success depends on it.

Section II: The Key Ingredients

27

Learn the compelling needs of your target audience.

28

The starting point of every successful sales campaign is knowing which challenges the buyer is compelled to solve.

29

Knowing the characteristics of your highest payoff prospects enables you to make good choices in planning and execution.

Section II: The Key Ingredients

30

Doing your homework enables you to craft a plan that propels your success.

31

Having powerful, insightful allies (in the account and via partners) makes your job much easier.

32

Use the new market research tools or you'll be blind-sided by not having information you need.

Section II: The Key Ingredients

33

Use the appropriate social networking tools for your industry to accelerate your efforts.

34

Pick a few new tools to add to your quiver. Try them. If they work, add them to your game plan.

35

Build your plan around your strengths, weaknesses, opportunities, and threats (SWOT).

36

Having good relationships are helpful, but to win, you must show that you deliver the best value.

Section II: The Key Ingredients

37

A well-respected, connected partner can make your job much easier and greatly shorten your sales cycle.

38

If you're not networking, you're playing with one hand tied behind your back.

39

When strategizing on an account, ask "How could we lose?" and fine-tune your plan.

40

"There are only two kinds of plans: Plans that won't work and plans that might work."
-General Wesley Clark

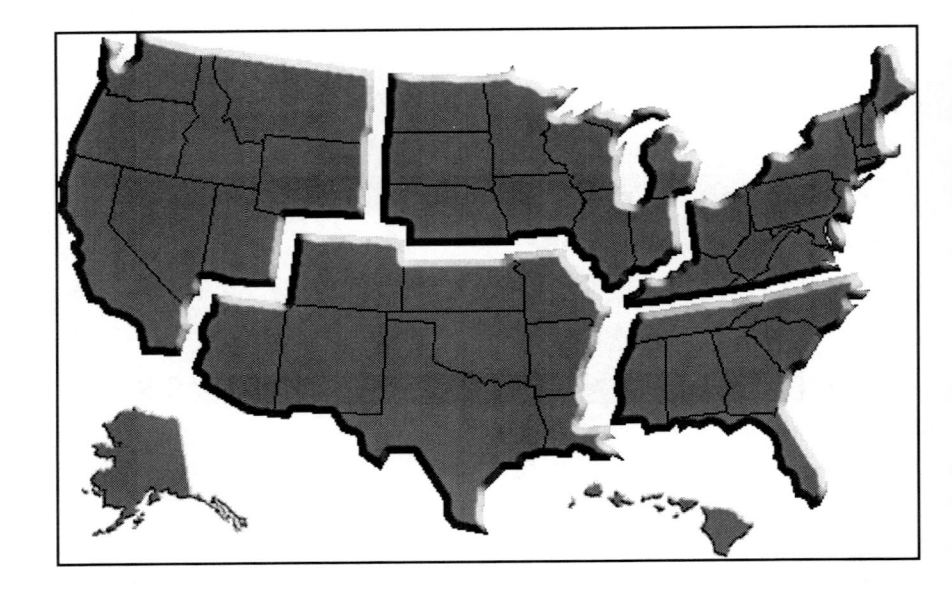

Section III: Penetrating Your Territory

Section III
Penetrating Your Territory

Practicing the techniques in this section will enable you to:
- Use market research to optimize your plan
- Employ and deploy the key elements of an effective territory plan
- Fill and manage your prospect funnel
- Calculate how many new opportunities you need to achieve your objective

To create a winning territory plan:
1. Start with market research.
2. Review your territory or vertical market. Identify logical groups of customers by territory, vertical industry or product needs and focus your plan on those segments.
3. Identify common problems within each customer segment and how your product/service solves them.
4. Conduct internet searches on your prospects' competitors to deepen your insight into your prospect's competitive vulnerabilities.
5. Review industry analysts' perspectives to ensure that your analysis is up to date and realistic.
6. Refer to Appendix D: Territory Planning Template.

With this in place, review information regarding your competitors and alternatives to your solution. This includes searching the web, your competitor's websites, market analyses of your offering, and both your company's and competitors' product literature. You must get beyond the hype—both from your company and your competitors.

Select the major points in each of the Strengths, Weaknesses, Opportunities, and Threats (SWOT) areas; these are the cornerstones of your plan. From these points, you then create strategies that enable you to capitalize on your strengths and opportunities in the marketplace. With strengths and opportunities defined, build out your plan to defend against your weaknesses and threats in the market.

Section III: Penetrating Your Territory

Capture the essence of your SWOT analysis in your value proposition. It clearly articulates how your advantages deliver value to the buyer of your products/services and how your offering is better than alternative solutions.

Next, do the math. Based on your goal, average sale, and conversion ratios, determine how many new opportunities you need to achieve your objectives. It is important that you know your conversion ratios (i.e. the percentage of unqualified leads that become qualified and the percentage of qualified leads that buy) and average sale size. With that information, you can calculate the number of leads and opportunities at each stage in the funnel you need to achieve your goal. (See the Funnel Requirement Formula in Appendix C.)

Then, to develop your territory penetration strategy, you must identify the characteristics of high-payoff customers and prospects. One of the hallmarks of successful sales organizations is that they have a system for identifying high-payoff accounts and opportunities. They clarify the characteristics of high probability opportunities and ruthlessly qualify so they spend their time and resources wisely.

Create a list of your top strategies. Use the characteristics of high-payoff prospects/customers to select your top accounts to pursue (see Appendix B for the list of Target Account Selection Criteria). Then, generate the list of your top opportunities which have both a compelling need for your product/service and represent enough business to warrant your attention. In some cases, the immediate business is relatively small, but it is worth pursuing to win the down-stream business. You need to be able to justify why each opportunity is on the list.

Next, identify the relationships you can leverage to fill your funnel and implement your plan successfully. Enlist the help of current customers to penetrate their account further and to contact their colleagues elsewhere who can use your products/services. List partners and other people who call on the same types of accounts. Include in your plan, how you will contact them and agree to support each other's business development efforts.

When using your network to look for leads, be specific about the characteristics of your high-payoff prospects. Your networking plan must include the appropriate social networking vehicles for your industry. For example, LinkedIn is great for business to business (B to B) networking. Facebook is good for business to consumer and personal networking (and gaining popularity in the B to B space).

Build on your success. Your plan must include how to leverage your happy customers to help you move buyers through their buying process. Buyers want to hear from other buyers. These sources are much more credible to them than information from sales people. Generate testimonials and case studies and other proof points for each stage of the sales cycle. Video is hot! A few thirty-second clips that clearly articulate the value you deliver can accelerate your sales process. One useful tool that makes it easy to produce and deliver video content is Brainshark.

Finally, an insightful plan helps you make the best use of your time and resources to produce the best possible results from your territory. Consistently monitor your progress against your plan and fine-tune your approach to win more business!

Self-Assessment

- Review your current territory plan. Given the suggestions in this chapter, how can you make the plan even better?
- What partners can you leverage to make it easier to penetrate deeper into current accounts and new prospects? What can you offer your partners to encourage them to help you?
- What relationships in your accounts can you nurture and leverage?
- What is your strategy to win each of your top opportunities?

Section III: Penetrating Your Territory

41

Don't kid yourself; thinking that you know everything that's going on in your territory.

42

Build a plan that takes advantage of the market opportunities in which you have unique strengths.

43

Don't believe the hype, yours or theirs. Do your research to know what is really going on.

44

Drive your strategy with a clear, compelling value proposition that articulates why someone should buy your product or service.

Section III: Penetrating Your Territory

45

Identify your niche and win it!

46

Your clear vision and strategy are the rallying point to focus your resources.

47

Good, buyer-focused marketing is the key to filling your funnel. You must coordinate your sales efforts with marketing.

Section III: Penetrating Your Territory

48

Ask yourself daily what you need to do to close your current opportunities.

49

Nurture your relationships; add value in every communication. This will help you identify and propel opportunities forward.

50
You must always keep your ear to the ground to identify new opportunities within your territory. It is so easy to miss a good one.

51
Vigilantly track your funnel. Do you have enough opportunities at your current conversion rates to make your goal?

Section III: Penetrating Your Territory

52
Focus on identifying opportunities early to influence decision criteria and greatly improve your probability of success.

53
There is nothing like a customer success story to get a new prospect's attention or push an interested party over the goal line.

54

Getting the most out of your territory is like solving a puzzle; once you've identified the most important parts, the rest falls in place.

Section III: Penetrating Your Territory

55

Video is HOT. Your plan needs to include using video testimonials and video sharing.

56

Collaborate with colleagues who sell to the same accounts. Leveraging each other's contacts expands your presence exponentially.

57

The measure of a person's presence has shifted from the size of their Rolodex to the size of their network. Build yours!

58

Act like your plan will be successful. Your attitude is a self-fulfilling prophecy.

Section III: Penetrating Your Territory

59

An insightful plan enables you to improve your conversion rates, so you don't need as many opportunities to make your goal.

60

If you are not leveraging your partners and colleagues in the territory you're leaving money on the table!

Section IV: Winning a Strategic Account

Section IV
Winning a Strategic Account

Mastering the steps in this section will enable you to:
- Identify the challenges and initiatives critical to your target accounts/business units
- Penetrate new business units
- Marshal an effective account team

Good account management can improve the quality of the opportunities in your pipeline, the effectiveness of your efforts to win business and your ability to forecast accurately. In a 2010 TAS Group survey of over 2000 companies, forty-eight percent of companies said they were planning significant investment in account management improvement.[1]

Recognizing the account's key challenges and initiatives is the starting point of account planning (see the Account Plan Template in Appendix E). Go to the account's website. Review each business unit and product line. Identify potential problems with each and how your product/service can solve them. Research their industry and top three to five competitors to deepen your insight into how you can help your prospect with their competitive challenges. With this analysis of the account/business unit in place, generate your SWOT list to formulate your account strategy and value proposition.

There are three fundamental ways to penetrate a key account.
1. In a new prospect, identify a compelling need that is aligned with the account's/business unit's key initiatives.
2. Within a business unit (BU) you are currently doing business with, look for opportunities to expand use of your product/service they are using and/or sell other products/services.
3. With a new BU in a current account, leverage your current sponsors and relationships to identify and be credible in new opportunities.

---

1. The TAS Group, "Great Account Management" (white paper) (2010), 2, http://www.thetasgroup.com/whitepaper/greataccountmgmt.html.

Section IV: Winning a Strategic Account

Your plan must demonstrate how your solution best addresses the issues and initiatives of the BU you are targeting. Further, you must show how you respond to the specific needs of each of the key buying influences in the decision process.

Track the total value of all opportunities to make sure you have sufficient opportunities in your funnel. As noted in Chapter 3, you need to track your conversion ratios (i.e. the percentage of leads for qualified opportunities that convert to sales and the number of unqualified leads that become qualified leads) and average size sale within this account, or accounts like it. With that, calculate the number of leads you need to have to achieve your goal. (See Appendix C for the Funnel Requirement Formula.)

High-performing sales organizations ensure that account teams work effectively across their company to win and serve strategic accounts. Just as in sports, you need selective player assignments to make the best use of the time and resources available. For example, having the right technical resources is a must in a technology-driven, solution sale. Further, leveraging the right partners can make a huge difference. This includes people who can alert you to new opportunities, those who can get you in the door, and those who can help you win.

Creating executive relationships between senior management in the customer's organization and yours is critical, especially in larger accounts. Miller Heiman's "Secrets of High Performing Sales Organizations" (2006),[2] indicated that seventy-seven percent of winning sales organizations (WSOs) said their senior-level executives actively promote and participate in the sales process, which is twenty percent more often than non-WSOs. A clear strategy is fundamental to enrolling and utilizing these valuable executive resources to keep your plan on track.

Success Story: Pre-Call Planning

Eric Doner, one of the authors, was well into his sales career before he grasped the value and enjoyed the benefits of proper pre-call planning. He says:

> I really got on board when I learned that calls turn out about the way you plan for them to. I formed the habit of capturing and reviewing the following information (in addition to names, titles, and buying roles) for each selling opportunity.

---

2. Miller Heiman, "Secrets of High Performing Sales Organizations," Miller Heiman Sales Performance Journal (2006): 6.

1. **Background information:** Make notes on account history, events leading up to the call, and possible customer needs.
2. **Call objective(s):** Set a realistic, desired outcome for each call and a back-up objective to continue the sales cycle.
3. **Call script:** Write what to say to open the call, build rapport, and bridge into a discussion/interview. Why risk "winging it"?
4. **Key questions:** Create a list of issues you need to learn more about. Balance open and closed questions to ensure an interview—and not an interrogation.
5. **Anticipated obstacles and solutions:** Consider the likely objections and how you can respond. Don't be blind-sided.
6. **Evidence and proofs:** Select sales aids and customer testimonials that can help make a case with a prospect/customer.
7. **Additional products/services:** List opportunities to up-sell or cross-sell when appropriate.

It takes discipline to follow this process on every call but the payoff from preparation can be huge! Calls often go as planned—and sometimes better! I've had calls that went so well that it was like the prospect had a copy of my plan. They readily answered all my questions, acknowledged that my solution met their needs, had no objections, and eagerly agreed to buy. It's a lesson I've never forgotten and a practice from which I never deviate.

Self-Assessment

- Review a current account plan. What can you do to make the plan even better?
- How can you better leverage your current contacts inside and outside the account?
- What additional partners can help you?
- Who else in your company can help you improve the plan and its implementation?
- What is your account team's greatest weakness? Who could help you in this area?
- Do you have broad coverage in the account? For example, what if a key player in the account changes jobs or leaves the company?
- Lack of account knowledge is the biggest inhibitor to success. What are you doing to ensure that you know what opportunities are emerging?

Section IV: Winning a Strategic Account

61

"The ability to gain victory by changing and adapting according to your opponent (situation) is called Genius."

-Sun Tzu, The Art of War

62

Decision makers want to do business with business people—not salespeople.

63

Every successful account plan requires that you understand and can satisfy your customer's needs.

Section IV: Winning a Strategic Account

64

You've got to be like a "recon scout"— to learn what is about to happen before it happens.

65

Show customers that you understand their business and can help solve important problems better than the other solution.

66

Implementing your plan is much easier if you've built a strong account team.

67

Everyone thinks their business is unique. Show them you understand their unique challenges.

Section IV: Winning a Strategic Account

68

To get the interest of executive decision makers, talk about what they don't know or don't know how to do.

69

Keeping your funnel filled with viable opportunities is critical.

70

Winning a major account is like playing a high stakes chess game; you must plan out your moves and anticipate competitive actions.

Section IV: Winning a Strategic Account

71

To be credible with decision makers you must know their marketplace and key initiatives.

72

Relationships are important but customers are buying value. Make sure you deliver.

73

If your funnel is weak, review your prospecting plan and the characteristics of the opportunities you are pursuing.

Section IV: Winning a Strategic Account

74

If your forecasts are not accurate, work on your sales process and account planning methods to improve predictability of your efforts.

75

Identify where you get stuck in the account management process and close any gaps to avoid being derailed.

76

As the account manager, you must ensure that everyone is working on the same action plan and have the resources they need.

Section IV: Winning a Strategic Account

77

If your team is not collaborating, sharing the plan and information, you are giving your competitor an easy advantage.

78

Including key internal players and partners will enhance your strategy and probability of success.

79

If you know where your offering is better and execute effectively, you will win more than your competitors.

80

Fish in the areas where the fish love your bait—where your unique competence gives you an "unfair advantage."

Section V: Managing Your Territory and Time

Section V
Managing Your Territory and Time

By implementing the practices outlined in this section you will be able to:
- Increase sales potential through improved geographic/market segment coverage
- Follow proven practices to establish sales territories
- Develop an annual sales call allocation plan
- Reduce sales costs through better travel and time management
- Improve ROI and sales force satisfaction through improved return on sales effort

The factors that affect setting up workable sales territories are: total number of accounts, account value, geography, time, and resources. If you find that your sales team cannot effectively cover all accounts in a territory, consider using alternative sales channels to reduce selling costs and reach a broader market. These include telemarketing, inside sales, and distributors.

After you have assessed the sales potential of your territory, set your revenue goals, rank your accounts and plan your selling tactics. Calculate how much time is required to sustain and grow your A accounts. Then, estimate how much time you need to spend to service your B accounts and grow them into A customers. Use whatever time remains to either develop your C accounts or cultivate new A and B prospects. We've provided a Sales Call Allocation Calculator in Appendix G to help with this task.

If you determine that you don't have the time or resources to make your numbers, discuss the situation with your manager or engage additional resources to help you.

Travel can be a huge drain on your time. On the other hand, you can be productive when flying or riding on a train by reviewing account information, preparing for your calls, or researching industries and new prospects. When driving, you can optimize "windshield time" and simultaneously sharpen your skills by listening to news on business trends that affect your customers or educational programs that can enhance your success. In a phone conversation, Mark Ramm, President of Tape Rental Library, told Doner, "Audio learning is the only kind of learning you can do while you're doing something else."

Section V: Managing Your Territory and Time

When you work in sales, you can divide your time into five basic categories:
1. **Face/connect:** in-person or on the phone connecting with prospects and customers.
2. **Research/planning:** studying industry/company trends and pre-call strategy.
3. **Phone/email:** attempts to connect with accounts, set appointments and follow up.
4. **Travel:** driving or riding in a cab, bus, train, or plane.
5. **Downtime:** time lost to interruptions, distractions, unplanned events, and bad habits.

According to Albert Gray, in a speech titled "The Common Denominator of Success" presented to The National Association of Life Underwriters in 1940, "The four success habits in selling are: prospecting habits, calling habits, selling habits, and working habits. If you take care of the first three, your work habits will take care of themselves."

Today, technology is the great enabler that can be applied to every stage of the sales process, from territory and account planning to closing the sale and servicing customers. For example, there are territory and account planning tools that enhance Customer Relationship Management (CRM) applications and reside within Salesforce.com. Teleconferencing, video conferencing, podcasts, webinars, and web meetings enable live interaction and the ability to share information and images with customers. And finally, smartphones and tablets provide mobile means to do almost everything you need to do!

Self-Assessment

- Think of how much time you have spent driving, waiting for meetings, etc. How could you have used that time more productively?
- Reflect on times when you have worked on B and C accounts when you could have been working on A accounts. How can you re-prioritize your actions? Keep a time log. You'll be surprised how you spend your time. (See the Sales Time Log in Appendix F.)
- Think of how much time you have spent on tasks that were not important or urgent. How could you use your time more effectively in the future?
- How could you work smarter? What new routine can you put in place that would significantly improve your efficiency?
- When driving in your territory, how could you plan a more efficient route to save time, save fuel, or visit more accounts?
- What could you do to more readily gain access to key people in your target accounts?

81

Control how you use your time. If you don't, you are sabotaging your chance for success.

82

You can't manage time; you can only manage how you use it. Follow your plan and focus on priority accounts.

Section V: Managing Your Territory and Time

83

If your focus is on new business, plan your time to contact more prospects.

84

If your focus is on account development/retention, optimize your time connecting with customers.

85

There are only two kinds of activities; goal achieving and tension relieving. Which are you doing?

Section V: Managing Your Territory and Time

86

"Unless you consciously form good habits, you unconsciously form bad habits."
-Albert E.N. Gray

87

Make your travel time count. Plan your prospecting around your major accounts.

88

Have a plan B to make other calls when appointments are cancelled at the last minute.

89

Listen to industry podcasts or personal development programs while driving.

Section V: Managing Your Territory and Time

90

Use waiting time to review your game plan and intended call outcomes.

91

There are two methods; the inspiration and the perspiration method. Work smarter—not harder.

92

Take best practice and make it common practice.

93

Block your office time and chunk your tasks.

Section V: Managing Your Territory and Time

94

Stay on good terms with your inside team.

95

If you're not using web meetings to interact with buyers, you are wasting time and missing opportunities!

96

Use your customer's preferred communication mode (phone, email, text, etc.).

97

Build rapport quickly and then get to the point. You are dealing with busy people.

Section V: Managing Your Territory and Time

98

Verify that your call objective and time required is consistent with your customer's.

99
Yesterday is a cancelled check, tomorrow is a promissory note. Only today is legal tender and only now is negotiable.

100
"Coffee is for closers."
-Alex Baldwin in Glengarry Glen Ross

Section VI: The Role of Sales Management

Section VI
The Role of Sales Management

By following the guidelines outlined in this section, you will be able to:
- Describe success requirements and Key Performance Indicators (KPIs)
- Define the roles, goals, and actions necessary to execute and monitor your plans
- Manage performance—support and coach your sales people
- Conduct periodic reviews—learn from your losses and celebrate your wins

A McKinsey & Company study demonstrated that first-level sales managers have the greatest impact on sales results. They are close enough to see what is going on in the sales environment, directly guide the sales process, and can greatly support the sales effort. There are many important roles that sales managers play, including hiring the right people and developing them. We will focus on how managers can improve sales results by helping the team develop and implement good sales plans.

The central focus of strategy coaching is helping sales people develop and implement a solid territory and/or strategic account plan. Here, a manager can share his or her knowledge of the marketplace. Managers can advise on what typically works in a particular type of account, stage in the sales process, or with certain types of buyers. Finally, asking good questions and being a good listener are critical to effective coaching.

According to Phil Bush, Sales Coach for TAS Group,[3] sixty-three percent of organizations think their sales managers should spend thirty to forty percent of their time coaching sales reps, yet sixty-one percent of organizations spend less than twenty percent of their time coaching their reps. His studies show a high correlation between coaching and higher revenues and profits.

A note to managers: despite your experience, don't expect your sales people to do it the way you did. Set the objective and leave room for them to do it their way. First, things may have changed since you carried a bag. Second, you want to leave room for people to do things within their style, provided they get the job done. And third, if they fail, those are the lessons that stick. Obviously, if it's a critical opportunity, you may need to step in so they don't fail.

---

3. Phil Bush, "Sales Coach" (webinar, The TAS Group, March 15, 2011).

Section VI: The Role of Sales Management

In order to be an effective coach, it is necessary to know when to intervene. Review the territory and account plans at the start of each selling year and on a quarterly basis. Then, throughout the year, monitor important opportunities to:

- Verify that compelling needs have been established.
- Ensure that the team has effectively influenced the decision criteria and demonstrated how your solution fits the buyers' criteria.
- Respond promptly to buyer concerns that can derail your efforts.
- Assist with constructing the proposal/contract and closing the sale.

One of the critical functions of sales management is to clarify key performance indicators by which sales people are measured and rewarded. Often, there are too many goals and measures and people get confused about where to focus their efforts. Be sure your measures support the accomplishments and encourage the behaviors you want, and are aligned with your business objectives. Research shows that aligning sales performance metrics with business objectives is a primary characteristic of well-managed sales organizations.

Management support and attention is a requirement for the adoption of any new sales initiative. This applies to changing the selling process, adopting a new methodology, or using a new sales force automation tool. Without management support, most change efforts fail. On the other hand, when management is fully engaged and on board, the probability of success is high.

Another major role of the sales manager is to ensure sufficient coordination and collaboration between sales and marketing. A survey by the CMO Council shows that less than twenty percent of respondents said their sales and marketing groups were "extremely collaborative," while most others felt that the two groups had "intermittent relations and interactions." Sales needs to be in synch with the markets that product development and marketing are targeting to fully leverage the company's differentiators and strategic direction. Marketing needs to support the sales effort by building market awareness, generating leads and nurturing immature leads. Therefore, marketing needs to know the market segments and key accounts sales is targeting. The hand-off between marketing and sales needs to be quick and easy to respond effectively to hot leads.

#PLAN to WIN tweet

There are tools that can help you respond appropriately to prospects inquiring about your offering. These range from simple auto-responders to marketing automation software, which provide lead ranking and customized responses to inquirers based on their behavior. It is important that sales and marketing are in agreement about lead ranking parameters, the definition of a "sales-ready" lead and how to make the hand-off between sales and marketing.

Finally, using a common CRM tool with appropriate access to information across the team goes a long way to enabling sales and marketing coordination. Further, there are collaboration tools that make it easy to gather input, share ideas, and enable everyone to keep up-to-date on the status of relevant projects.

Self-Assessment

- Reflect on recent territory/account reviews. What usable ideas did your reps get from the session? How can you provide more value in territory/account reviews?
- How can you encourage the team to provide better feedback to their peers?
- Reflect on a time in which the coordination between sales and marketing was poor. What were the consequences? What can you do to improve coordination in the future?
- What tools could help you improve the coordination between sales and marketing?
- What tools can you use to manage the team more effectively?
- Who can mentor you to take your coaching abilities to the next level?

Section VI: The Role of Sales Management

101

Territory/account reviews must give sales reps useful ideas that help win business. Otherwise, it's a useless exercise.

102

Top performers seek and need feedback; provide insight to your reps on what they don't see.

103

First line to executive management support is crucial to the successful implementation of territory and account planning.

Section VI: The Role of Sales Management

104

Have your people demonstrate how they are using their tools. Management involvement is critical reinforcement.

105

Marshal your team's collective knowledge by sharing and using best practices.

106

Brainstorm with your sales team to find solutions to their biggest challenges.

Section VI: The Role of Sales Management

107

Know when to intervene in the sales cycle and when to provide coaching/guidance.

108

Coaching must be very clear and specific to improve performance.

109

Model the behavior you seek from your team.

Section VI: The Role of Sales Management

110

Identify what your reps are missing, help them see it, and guide them on how to correct it.

111

Dropping the ball in the hand-off between Marketing and Sales can cost you the sale.

112

Sales and Marketing must agree on the definition of a "sales-ready" lead and use it to drive lead generation efforts.

113

Marketing must provide "sales-ready" leads and sales must follow up on them immediately.

Section VI: The Role of Sales Management

114

Promote and support the tools available to your team. These tools are productivity multipliers.

115

Feedback accelerates your learning curve and provides insights you cannot see yourself.

116

Ask for feedback from your management, colleagues, partners, prospects, and customers.

Section VI: The Role of Sales Management

117

The days of the lone ranger are long gone. In large complex sales, the best sales team wins.

118

When you win as a team, there is plenty of credit to go around. When you lose on your own, it's clear who is responsible.

119

Break through internal and external road blocks to ensure your plan succeeds.

120

The top athletes and teams have coaches for a reason... they improve performance!

Section VII: Executing Your Plan

Section VII
Executing Your Plan

By implementing the steps described in this section you will be able to:
- Recognize and avoid the pitfalls that prevent successful plan execution
- Practice agility and flexibility to achieve your goals
- Demonstrate the discipline required to win
- Identify the type of tools you need to improve performance

At the end of the day, a plan is only as good as its execution. There are countless stories of great ideas and good plans that have not produced anything. If you want your plan to produce your intended results, you must actively and consistently drive its execution. A *Harvard Business Review* article, "Beware the Busy Manager" (2002)[4] summarizes a ten-year management study. They found that fully ninety percent of managers squander their time in all sorts of ineffective activities. Or as Doner says, "There is a big difference between business and busyness. Don't confuse activity with accomplishment."

You must identify the key actions within each stage in the sales process for each opportunity. Typically, there are one or two stages in which progress slows or even stalls. Identify the primary cause(s) and put a plan in place to respond. As the decision process heats up—in the selection phase—the plan must be reviewed and adjusted more often.

You need to monitor progress and fine-tune your approach so you can make adjustments before it is too late! In addition to measuring the key outcomes on which you are graded (i.e. sales production), you need to track leading indicators that can be measured before the sale is won or lost, such as:
- Are you generating enough leads to make your goal?
- Are your conversion ratios at each stage of the process where they need to be to make the most of the opportunities you have?
- Are you achieving advances (is the prospect committing to do something to move the sale forward in a specific timeframe) with each interaction?
- Are you getting the right people involved?

---

4. Heike Bruch and Sumantra Ghoshal, "Beware the Busy Manager, Harvard Business Review, (February 2002).

Section VII: Executing Your Plan

Managing relationships can be tricky. Sometimes players change allegiance mid-stream. Other times, people run hot and cold. You need to be flexible and adjust on the fly. Further, you must be vigilant to identify and respond to the needs of new key players, new initiatives, and changing perspectives as the sales process unfolds. This will enable you to nimbly respond to changes as they emerge.

Are you taking advantage of the modern technology available to improve your team's efficiency? Sales force automation, including Salesforce.com and Oracle CRM On Demand, and file sharing tools, like Basecamp, help teams to respond to prospects and customers more quickly and effectively. Social networking sites, i.e. LinkedIn, Facebook and Twitter, enable you to leverage your contacts, identify new prospects, and get support to advance your sales process. Other tools that enable you to gather targeted contact information include Inside View, Jigsaw, Demandbase. and LinkSV. Google and Yahoo! Alerts as well as industry and technology sites/blogs/newsletters can give you an edge in responding to new opportunities. Finally, there are marketing automation tools, such as Marketo and Eloqua, that help you rank leads and respond appropriately based on buyer behavior.

Effective implementation requires persistent focus and consistent monitoring. This improves results in critical success factors, such as revenue production, sales cycle length, and average selling price. It also improves sales per sales person and forecast performance/predictability—key sales management measures.

Self-Assessment

- Review your current plan. What can you do to make it more effective? What resources (internal and external) can you enlist to make it easier to implement the plan?
- Reflect on how you execute your plan. What can you do differently that will accelerate your results?
- Look at your team and how well it operates. Do you need to add someone to the team? Do you need to change player assignments?
- Review how well you manage each stage in the sales process. Identify one or two stages in which you often get stuck. What is the key stumbling block? What can you do to overcome it?

- Which automation tools are you using? Identify one or two areas where a new tool could have significant impact on your results. Research and try new tools in those areas.
- Do your territory/account plans reside in your sales force automation (SFA) tool? If not, identify a tool to support your planning and implementation process.
- Are you using measures that don't contribute to your performance that you can eliminate?
- Are you measuring leading indicators that tell you if you are on target, before the opportunity is won or lost?

Section VII: Executing Your Plan

121

You can't always get what you want, but if you inspect, you will get what you expect.

122

Planning is the breakfast of champions. Focus on your most important tasks each day.

123

Without a vision, you're likely to wander and not make it to the promised land.

124

Review your plan regularly... and use it to guide your actions.

Section VII: Executing Your Plan

125

Ideas are a dime a dozen; putting them to use is priceless.

126

Delegate to your team. Your role is to get the job done. You don't have to do it yourself.

127

Use the right person—with the right skill set—for each job and your chances of winning go up dramatically.

Section VII: Executing Your Plan

128

Use your plan to keep your eye on the prize. It's easy to get distracted.

129

Your plan needs to be a living document; update and fine-tune it regularly.

130

"Things may come to those who wait, but only the things left by those who hustle." -Abraham Lincoln

131

"Adaptating means not clinging to fixed methods, but changing according to events, acting as is suitable." -Sun Tzu, The Art of War

Section VII: Executing Your Plan

132

At the end of every sales call, review what went well and what could be done differently. This step will greatly improve future results.

133

Review and fine-tune your plan more frequently as the decision process heats up to respond to rapidly changing conditions.

134

Track key performance indicators. Watch them like a hawk. Identify issues and respond quickly!

Section VII: Executing Your Plan

135

Listen more than you talk; pay close attention to your customers and verify what you heard.

136

Confirm your appointments so you don't travel to a meeting that doesn't happen. Update your CRM ASAP after each call.

137

In so many markets, buyers see competitive offerings as largely the same. Here, a good plan and excellent execution will win.

138

Eighty percent of the value comes from twenty percent of your effort. How can you make the other eighty percent more effective?

Section VII: Executing Your Plan

139

"Hope is not a Strategy."
-Rick Page

140

"There's no such thing as the perfect plan; you have to take a plan that might work and make it work."
-Gen. Wesley Clark

Appendix A: Territory and Account Planning Resources

Territory and Account Planning Software Tools

- *Territory Plan Pro*: territory planning application by Plan 2 Win Software
- *Account Plan Pro*: strategic account planning application by Plan 2 Win Software
- *Pre Call Planning*: pre-call planning by Plan 2 Win Software
- *ProAlign*: territory alignment and optimization software by Mapping Analytics
- *Territory Mapper and AlignStar*: territory mapping software by TTG, Inc.
- *Tactician*: product line for territory design by Tactician Corp.
- *TerrAlign*: territory design by TerrAlign Group
- *VueWise Territory Maps* by VueWise

Reading for Extra Credit

1. Bacon, Terry R. *Selling to Major Accounts: Tools, Techniques, and Practical Solutions for the Sales Manager.* New York: American Management Association, 1999.
2. Bosworth, Michael T., Holland, John R., and Visgatis, Rank. *CustomerCentric Selling* (second edition), New York: McGraw-Hill, 2010.
3. Covey, Stephen, Merrill, A. Roger, and Merrill, Rebecca R. *First Things First.* New York: Simon & Schuster, 1994.
4. Feigon, Josiane Chriqui. *Smart Selling on the Phone and Online: Inside Sales That Get Results.* New York: American Management Association, 2010.
5. Kahle, Dave. *10 Secrets of Time Management for Salespeople: Gain the Competitive Edge and Make Every Second Count.* Franklin Lakes, NJ: Career Press, 2003.
6. Konrath, Jill. *Selling to Big Companies.* Chicago: Dearborn Trade Publishing, 2006.
7. Miller, Robert B., Heiman, Stephen E., and Tujela Tad. *The New Successful Large Account Management: Maintaining and Growing your Most Important Assets – Your Customers.* New York: Warner Business Books, 2005.

Strategic Territory and Account Planning

8. Ott, Adrian C. *The 24-Hour Customer: New Rules for Winning in a Time-Starved, Always-Connected Economy.* New York: HarperBusiness, 2010.
9. Page, Rick. *Hope is Not a Strategy: the 6 Keys to Winning the Complex Sale.* New York: Nautilus Press, 2002.
10. Rackham, Neil, and DeVincentis, John R. *Rethinking the Sales Force: Redefining Selling to Create and Capture Customer Value.* New York: McGraw-Hill, 1999.
11. Seley, Anneke, and Holloway, Brent. *Sales 2.0: Improve Business Results Using Innovative Sales Practices and Technology.* Hoboken, NJ: John Wiley & Sons, Inc., 2009.
12. Simpkins, Robert A. *The Secrets of Great Sales Management: Advanced Strategies for Maximizing Performance.* New York: American Management Association, 2004.
13. Stevenson, Tom, and Barcus, Sam. *The Relationship Advantage: Become a Trusted Advisor and Create Clients for Life.* Chicago: Dearborn, 2003.
14. Ursiny, Timothy E., and DeMoss, Gary. *Coaching the Sale: Discover the Issues, Discuss Solutions and Decide an Outcome!.* Naperville, IL: Sourcebooks, 2006.
15. Vanella, Mari Anne. *42 Rules of Cold Calling Executives.* Cupertino, CA: Superstar Press, 2008.

Useful Websites

- Plan 2 Win Software – Sales Enablement Tools, http://www.TerritoryPlan.com
- Achievement Training Associates, http://www.AchieveCorp.com
- Breakthrough Inc., http://www.Breakthrough-Inc.com
- Link Silicon Valley (LinkSV), http://www.LinkSV.com
- Compendian, http://www.Compendian.com
- Sales Training Camp, http://www.SalesTrainingCamp.com
- Selling to Big Companies, http://www.SellingtoBigCompanies.com
- Washburn Endeavors, LLC, http://www.WashburnEndeavours.com
- Vanella Group, http://www.VanellaGroup.com
- Phone Works, http://www.PhoneWorks.com

- TeleSmart, http://www.Tele-Smart.com
- Industry Gems, http://www.IndustryGems.com

Professional Sales Associations

Sales & Marketing Executives International (SMEI) is the professional association for sales and marketing. http://www.smei.org

Strategic Account Management Association (SAMA) is the profession's leading source of comprehensive trend and research information. The association provides its members with the training, knowledge, and networking opportunities required to successfully manage strategic account programs. http://strategicaccounts.org

The Professional Society for Sales & Marketing Training (SMT) is the ONLY association fully dedicated to accelerating business results for its member organizations by improving sales and marketing performance through training. http://www.SMT.org

Strategic Territory and Account Planning

Appendix B: Target Account Selection Criteria

The ten questions below comprise the criteria that can help you analyze your probability of success with a target account.

1. **Product fit:** How well do your product/service capabilities align with the customer's technical and business requirements?
2. **Business alignment:** What is the short and long-term profitability potential of the business relationship for both parties?
3. **Value/price ratio:** How price sensitive is the target account? To what extent do they tend to emphasize value more than price?
4. **Customer urgency:** How pressing is the need to solve the problem, change suppliers, or pursue a different course of action? Is there a compelling event?
5. **Logistics:** How well are you able to meet customer logistical requirements, such as ability to meet availability/delivery requirements and fit in their space?
6. **Quality of information:** How good and accessible is information about the account—either publicly available or obtainable from inside?
7. **Alignment of influence:** How well are you aligned with those who influence and make the decision? How supportive are they of you, your offering, and your company?
8. **Quality of coaching/sponsorship:** Do you have opportunities to develop "coaches/sponsors?" Can you cultivate influential people inside who are willing to share important business and organizational information with you and willing to coach you on winning the business?
9. **Entrenched competition:** How strong is the allegiance to a competitive or internal solution? How determined are the people within the account who can restrict access to senior-level management, create obstacles and block or derail your strategy?
10. **Cultural fit:** How well does the target account align with your company's philosophies for buying based on value, open communication, and emphasis on building business partnerships?

Strategic Territory and Account Planning

Appendix C: Funnel Requirement Formula

Here is a formula for calculating how much business you need in your funnel to make your goals. Improving your effectiveness through good planning, implementation, and strategy coaching makes it possible to achieve your goals with less fewer opportunities in your funnel.

Funnel Requirement

(1 / Win Ratio) x Average Cycle Length x Target Sales

Win Ratio = % of opportunities pursued that are won

Average Sales Cycle Length = average time it takes to win an opportunity

Quarterly Funnel Requirement Example:

1 / (50% close ratio)	x	(6 months to close / 3 months/ qtr.)	x	($1M/ year/4 qtrs./yr.)
need 2 to get 1		need 2 to get 1		$250 K = $1M
2	x	2	x	$250 K = $1M

Annual Funnel Requirement Example:

1 / (50% close ratio)	x	(6 months to close / 12 months/ year)	x	($1M/ year)
need 2 to get 1		need 1/2 to get 1		$1M = $1M
2	x	1/2	x	$1M = $1M

Strategic Territory and Account Planning

The Impact of Improving Effectiveness

Example:

Improve your close ratio and the sales cycle length by 10% each and the Funnel Requirement decreases by 18%:

1 / (55% close ratio)	x	(5.4 months to close / 12 mo/ year)	x	($1M/ year)
1.82	x	.45	x	$1M = $.82M

Example:

Improve your close ratio and the sales cycle length by 20% each and the Funnel Requirement decreases by 33%:

1 / (60% close ratio)	x	(4.8 months to close / 12 mo/ year)	x	($1M/ year)
1.67	x	.4	x	$1M = $.67M

Appendix D: Territory Planning Template

Territory Information

What is happening in your industry?
What is occurring in your territory/ vertical market?

Your Strengths/Opportunities to Leverage

Trends in the industry, regulations, economy, geography and vertical market

1.
2.
3.

Your Weaknesses/Threats to Counter

Trends in the industry, regulations, economy, geography and vertical market

1.
2.
3.

Characteristics of Best Prospects

Characteristics of your best and worst customers

1.
2.
3.

Strategic Territory and Account Planning

Strategies
- Strategies to generate new opportunities
- Strategies to win opportunities in the funnel
- Partners, associations, colleagues to leverage

1.
2.
3.

Top Accounts
Current customers to grow and new prospects to win

Current Customers	New Prospects
1.	
2.	
3.	

Top Opportunities
Within customers and new prospects

Opportunity	Value you provide	$ Value of Opportunity
1.		
2.		
3.		
4.		
5.		

Appendix E: Strategic Account Planning Template

Account Information

Important aspects of the account's business

What is impacting their industry?
What is impacting them in your territory or vertical?
The account's key initiative to leverage:
What is their budget, decision process?

Your Strengths/ Opportunities to Leverage

Trends in the industry, regulations, economy, geography and vertical market

1.
2.
3.

Your Weaknesses/Threats to Counter

Trends in the industry, regulations, economy, geography and vertical market

1.
2.
3.

Strategic Territory and Account Planning

Characteristics of Best Opportunities

Characteristics of your most and least successful projects

1.
2.
3.

Strategies

1. Strategies to generate new opportunities
2. Strategies to win opportunities in the funnel
3. Partners, associations, colleagues to leverage

1.
2.
3.

Relationships to Leverage

People in the account, internal people, partners, and others who call on the account

	Relationship	Relationship Strategy
1.		
2.		

Top Opportunities

In business units you do business with and new ones

	Opportunity	Value you provide	$ Value of Opportunity
1.			
2.			
3.			

Appendix F: Sales Time Log

Day/date:						How to use this time log:
Daily Activity	Face/Face or Connected phone calls	Research & Planning	Call attempts & email	Travel	Downtime	The goal is to help you see how you spend your time so that you can use it more profitably.
						1. Make several printed copies of this form to use over several days.
7:30 AM						2. You can annotate the log or use the spreadsheet if you prefer.
8:00 AM						
8:30 AM						
9:00 AM						3. Time is shown in thirty-minute blocks to keep things simple.
9:30 AM						
10:00 AM						
10:30 AM						4. Enter an "X" in the box that reflects how you used your time in each block.
11:00 AM						
11:30 AM						
12:00 PM						
12:30 PM						5. If you engaged in more than one activity in one time block, check each.
1:00 PM						
1:30 PM						
2:00 PM						You may also want to show what portion (10, 15, 20) you used for each activity.
2:30 PM						
3:00 PM						

Strategic Territory and Account Planning

Time						
3:30 PM						
4:00 PM						
4:30 PM						
5:00 PM						
5:30 PM						
6:00 PM						
6:30 PM						
7:00 PM						
7:30 PM						

6. Keep track of how you use your time for several days to see if patterns evolve.

7. Make adjustments as necessary to maximize your productivity and increase your selling time.

8. Good Luck and Good Selling!

Appendix G: Annual Sales Call Allocation Calculator

1. Calculate how many selling days you really have in a year.

	You	Example
Number of workdays in a typical year:	260	260
Subtract for # recognized holidays		10
Less your vacation days (10–15?)		10
Less personal days (jury duty, sick days)		10
Less company meetings, trade shows and conferences		12
Subtract "firefighting" (special service calls, etc.)		3
Total # days to subtract	_____	-45
Equals total # days available for personal selling:		215

2. How many face-face calls can you make a day (on average)? — 4

3. Calculate # calls you have available annually:

Example: 4 calls/day X 215 calling days =	860	calls available

Strategic Territory and Account Planning

4. Consider this example to budget 860 available sales calls:	# accounts	# calls required	Total # calls
# Key accounts - 'A' customers	60	10	600
# Target high-value 'A' prospects	30	8	240
# 'B' customers	25	5	125
# 'B' prospects	14	3	42
Total # calls committed			**1007**
Less Total # calls available			**-860**
Equals # calls available to pursue other sales opportunities:			**-147** *

5. Determine how you will allocate your calls.	# accounts	# calls required	Total # calls
# Key accounts - 'A' customers			
# Target high-value 'A' prospects			
# 'B' customers			
# 'B' prospects			
Total # calls committed			_____
Less Total # calls available			_____
Equals # calls available to pursue other sales opportunities:			

* In the example, the seller is over-committed by 147 calls on current prospects and customers, and has no extra calls available to pursue new opportunities. This will require re-assessment of the number of calls required to sell or retain each type of account. Consider these kinds of questions: Can you really make four calls/day? Does every A customer require ten calls/year? Can some B accounts be handed off to inside sales to further qualify or service? Once your budget is realistic you can confidently execute the proper number of calls you really need to make to achieve your account and territory goals.

Good Luck and Good Selling!

About the Authors

Ron Snyder is President of Plan2Win Software, providing territory, account and pre-call planning applications that run in SalesForce.com, and Breakthrough, Inc, a sales consultancy that enables companies to accelerate sales by improving sales effectiveness. For over twenty years, Ron has helped companies improve results in competitive, high-value, complex selling environments. Before that, at Hewlett-Packard, Ron was a top-ranked sales person, manager in the field sales organization and a marketing manager, bringing products to market. He has also worked as a product designer and engineering project manager. Ron holds a Bachelors Degree and Masters Degree in Engineering Design from Tufts University and an MBA from Northeastern University.

Strategic Territory and Account Planning

Eric Doner is the founder of Achievement Training Associates, a consulting firm that helps organizations align and leverage people and processes to improve performance. His career spans over twenty-five years of success in sales, marketing and training & development. Eric has held positions with Dun & Bradstreet, BASF, Compuware and the American Management Association. He served as President of the Silicon Valley American Marketing Association and Sales & Marketing Executives of Cleveland, OH. Eric has published articles and led seminars on Sales Management, Sales Coaching and Customer-Focused Selling. He earned his BSBA at Bowling Green State University and completed postgraduate work in adult learning, human performance development and instructional technology.

Other Books in the THiNKaha Series

The THiNKaha book series is for thinking adults who lack the time or desire to read long books, but want to improve themselves with knowledge of the most up-to-date subjects. THiNKaha is a leader in timely, cutting-edge books and mobile applications from relevant experts that provide valuable information in a fun, Twitter-brief format for a fast-paced world.

They are available online at http://thinkaha.com or at other online and physical bookstores.

1. *#BOOK TITLE tweet Book01:* 140 Bite-Sized Ideas for Compelling Article, Book, and Event Titles by Roger C. Parker
2. *#BUSINESS SAVVY PM tweet Book01:* Project Management Mindsets, Skills, and Tools for Generating Successful Business Results by Cinda Voegtli
3. *#COACHING tweet Book01:* 140 Bite-Sized Insights On Making A Difference Through Executive Coaching by Sterling Lanier
4. *#CONTENT MARKETING tweet Book01:* 140 Bite-Sized Ideas to Create and Market Compelling Content by Ambal Balakrishnan
5. *#CORPORATE CULTURE tweet Book01:* 140 Bite-Sized Ideas to Help You Create a High Performing, Values Aligned Workplace that Employees LOVE by S. Chris Edmonds
6. *#CROWDSOURCING tweet Book01:* 140 Bite-Sized Ideas to Leverage the Wisdom of the Crowd by Kiruba Shankar and Mitchell Levy
7. *#DEATHtweet Book01:* A Well-Lived Life through 140 Perspectives on Death and Its Teachings by Timothy Tosta
8. *#DEATH tweet Book02:* 140 Perspectives on Being a Supportive Witness to the End of Life by Timothy Tosta
9. *#DIVERSITYtweet Book01:* Embracing the Growing Diversity in Our World by Deepika Bajaj

Strategic Territory and Account Planning

10. *#DREAMtweet Book01:* Inspirational Nuggets of Wisdom from a Rock and Roll Guru to Help You Live Your Dreams by Joe Heuer
11. *#ENTRYLEVELtweet Book01:* Taking Your Career from Classroom to Cubicle by Heather R. Huhman
12. *#ENTRY LEVEL tweet Book02:* Relevant Advice for Students and New Graduates in the Day of Social Media by Christine Ruff and Lori Ruff
13. *#EXPERT EXCEL PROJECTS tweet:* Taking Your Excel Project From Start To Finish Like An Expert by Larry Moseley
14. *#IT OPERATIONS MANAGEMENT tweet Book01:* Managing Your IT Infrastructure in The Age of Complexity by Peter Spielvogel, Jon Haworth, Sonja Hickey
15. *#JOBSEARCHtweet Book01:* 140 Job Search Nuggets for Managing Your Career and Landing Your Dream Job by Barbara Safani
16. *#LEADERSHIPtweet Book01:* 140 Bite-Sized Ideas to Help You Become the Leader You Were Born to Be by Kevin Eikenberry
17. *#LEADS to SALES tweet Book01:* Creating Qualified Business Leads in the 21st Century by Jim McAvoy
18. *#LEAN SIX SIGMA tweet Book01:* Business Process Excellence for the Millennium by Dr. Shree R. Nanguneri
19. *#LEAN STARTUP tweet Book01:* 140 Insights for Building a Lean Startup! by Seymour Duncker
20. *#MILLENNIALtweet Book01:* 140 Bite-Sized Ideas for Managing the Millennials by Alexandra Levit
21. *#MOJOtweet:* 140 Bite-Sized Ideas on How to Get and Keep Your Mojo by Marshall Goldsmith
22. *#MY BRAND tweet Book01:* A Practical Approach to Building Your Personal Brand - 140 Characters at a Time by Laura Lowell
23. *#OPEN TEXTBOOK tweet Book01:* Driving the Awareness and Adoption of Open Textbooks by Sharyn Fitzpatrick
24. *#PARTNER tweet Book01:* 140 Bite-Sized Ideas for Succeeding in Your Partnerships by Chaitra Vedullapalli

#PLAN to WIN tweet

25. *#PLAN to WIN tweet Book01:* Strategic Territory and Account Planning by Ron Snyder and Eric Doner
26. *#PRESENTATION tweet Book01:* 140 Ways to Present with Impact by Wayne Turmel
27. *#PRIVACY tweet Book01:* Addressing Privacy Concerns in the Day of Social Media by Lori Ruff
28. *#PROJECT MANAGEMENT tweet Book01:* 140 Powerful Bite-Sized Insights on Managing Projects by Guy Ralfe and Himanshu Jhamb
29. *#QUALITYtweet Book01:* 140 Bite-Sized Ideas to Deliver Quality in Every Project by Tanmay Vora
30. *#RISK MANAGEMENT tweet Book01:* Proactive Risk Management: Taming Alligators by Cinda Voegtli & Laura Erkeneff
31. *#SCRAPPY GENERAL MANAGEMENT tweet Book01:* Practical Practices for Magnificent Management Results by Michael Horton
32. *#SOCIAL MEDIA PR tweet Book01:* 140 Bite-Sized Ideas for Social Media Engagement by Janet Fouts
33. *#SOCIALMEDIA NONPROFIT tweet Book01:* 140 Bite-Sized Ideas for Nonprofit Social Media Engagement by Janet Fouts with Beth Kanter
34. *#SPORTS tweet Book01:* What I Learned from Coaches About Sports and Life by Ronnie Lott with Keith Potter
35. *#STANDARDS tweet Book01:* 140 Bite-Sized Ideas for Winning the Industry Standards Game by Karen Bartleson
36. *#TEAMWORK tweet Book01:* Lessons for Leading Organizational Teams to Success 140 Powerful Bite-Sized Insights on Lessons for Leading Teams to Success by Caroline G. Nicholl
37. *#THINKtweet Book01:* Bite-Sized Lessons for a Fast Paced World by Rajesh Setty
38. *#TOXINS tweet Book01:* 140 Easy Tips to Reduce Your Family's Exposure to Environmental Toxins by Laurel J. Standley Ph.D.

Strategic Territory and Account Planning

THiNK Continuity™ Training/Learning Program

THiNK Continuity™ delivers high-quality, cost-effective continuous learning in easy-to-understand, worthwhile, and digestible chunks. Fifteen minutes with a *THiNKaha*® book will allow the reader to have one or more "aha" moments. An hour and a half monthly with a THiNK Continuity program will allow the learner to have an opportunity to truly digest the topic being covered.

Offered online and/or in person, these engaging programs feature gurus (ours and yours) on such relevant topics as Leadership, Management, Sales, Marketing, Work-Life Balance, Project Management, Social Media and Networking, Presentation Skills, and other topics of your choosing. The "learning" audience, whether it is clients, employees or partners, can now experience high-quality learning that will enhance your brand value and empower your company as a thought leader. This program fits a real need where time and the high cost of developing custom content are no longer an option for every organization.

Just **THiNK**...

1. **C**ontinuous Employee/Client/Prospect Learning
2. **O**ngoing Thought Leadership Development
3. **N**otable Experts Presenting on Relevant Topics
4. **T**ime Your Attendees Can Afford – 15 min. to 2 hrs/mth
5. **I**nformation Delivered in Digestible Chunks
6. **N**ame the Topic – We Help You Provide Expert Best Practices
7. **U**nderstand and Implement the Takeaways
8. **I**nternal Expertise Shared Externally
9. **T**raining/Prospecting Cost Decreases, Effectiveness Increases
10. **Y**ou Win, They Win!

More Praises for *#PLAN to WIN tweet*

"Eric and Ron cover all of the things that have made them successful and have chosen to share their nuggets of knowledge with you, the reader. Good stuff that anyone and everyone can benefit from in today's fast-paced and hectic selling world."
Chuck Carey, CEO Compendian

"In today's sales landscape, the only actions that will fuel your sales efforts are creating and implementing a well thought out strategic territory and account plan—perfect timing for Ron Snyder and Eric Doner's *#PLAN to WIN tweet!* This is a must-have book to add to your sales warrior wisdom."
Josiane Feigon, Author of Smart Selling on the Phone and Online

---

"Managing a solid strategic accounts program requires a solid plan. Ability to implement this plan makes a huge difference in the outcome. This book helps you lay that foundation and the on-going relationship. These are key elements that I emphasize when working with my complex/strategic account managers and their corporate customers."
Victoria Hibbits, Vice President of Medical Imaging / Complex and Government Accounts McKesson Provider Technologies

---

"This book is a must read for sales managers and their sales people. Territory and account planning is necessary to get the most from your sales force automation. It gives you the depth you require to truly manage your business thoughtfully."
John Reighard, Owner of a sales consulting business, former Regional Sales Director and VP, Worldwide Sales Development of Exodus Communication

Strategic Territory and Account Planning

"Finally, a book that makes sense about the art of selling! This work provides true insight into the role of strategy and planning in good selling and shares excellent thoughts on effective execution. Great work guys!"

Dr. Ronald Fountain, Chairman of the Board of Trustees, MetroHealth System; Dean, Walsh University School of Business, Retired.

"*#PLAN to WIN tweet* is the perfect partner in helping you establish an unfair advantage. With the information that is easily accessible today, top performers have to plan prior to showing up or they will not gain the insight and, ultimately, the trust that buyers demand before placing the order. If you follow these key steps in every sale, you will be sure to take your sales career to another level."

Mark Miller, Vice President, Sales and Marketing, ZONARE Medical Systems